LET'S PLAY THESE *Games*

by Frances Lane

Illustrated throughout by Patrick Rose.
Cover by Ron Branagan.

Lane, Frances
Lets play these games
1. Children's games - Collections
I. Title
790.1'922

ISBN 0-948834-01-3

INTRODUCTION

These games have been collected, adapted and invented over several years with my Cub Pack and Scout Troop. Most of them have already been "field-tested" by the boys; and any of them can be further adapted to fit your own particular organisation. I have used the term 'he' throughout the book, although the games are, of course, equally suitable for boys or girls.

The games in this book are listed in alphabetical order, with some variations given beneath - I leave you to find others. Equipment needed for each game is also listed - that saves you from having to read the whole explanation, only to find that you can't play the game anyway because you lack some essential piece of equipment!

Each title is followed by a letter, or series of letters to indicate its category. To find a certain type of game, one only has to look at the letters.

S	Solo games - each boy against all the others
T	Team games
R	Relay games
L	Loop games - no winners, no losers, the game just goes on
TR	Training games (training in its wider sense of learning skills)
Q	Quiet games

XX Games for which no special equipment is needed. (If the place that you meet in is anything like mine, then such gear as these games require will be readily available - tables, chairs, ball etc.)

X Games for which no equipment at all is needed

An Index of all the games and their categories can be found at the back of the book.

I find the last category the most useful; when there's an unplanned five-minutes break in the proceedings, or when leaders have to be called away to cope with a sudden emergency, a game tagged 'X' means that it can be run there and then.

SETTING UP

I file my games on 5" x 3" index cards; each has two holes punched in the bottom so that they can be strung together; if they get dropped, they still stay in one piece. Filing in an ordinary card-file box makes it easier to add new games, but it does mean that they have to be individually resorted if the box is dropped.

Each card carries a standard notation, front and back:

FRONT		**BACK**
TITLE	CATEGORY	Q: (EQUIPMENT NEEDED)
RULES		DATES PLAYED (saves the same game from coming out too often)

Using this method, it is possible to tell the type of game, the gear needed, and the date it was last played, just by flicking through the cards.

Try not to have too many games where players are 'out'; they generally start an alternative game on the sidelines. We use 'lives' - one sleeve up, both sleeves up, and <u>then</u> out - and no game should go on long enough for more than a couple of players to lose all three lives and become a nuisance on the side lines. If you must have a winner, count it as the player who's lost the least lives.

We don't count a team as 'finished' until they're all lined up neatly, sitting or standing, depending upon how they started the game. In this case, we have awarded first place to the team who finished second, because they were the first to be lined up properly. It only has to be done once or twice for them all to get the message.

Unsportsmanlike behaviour should be suppressed at all costs. Winning should never be so important that it gets in the way of enjoyment. The point of a game <u>is</u> the game - and if the atmosphere is going to be spoiled by a win-at-all-costs mentality, then it isn't worth playing. Children have got to learn how to lose as well as how to win; it also won't do any harm for them to learn that there are worse things in life than losing fairly.

Make sure that the members (and other leaders!) are quiet while you're explaining a new game. Keep the rules short and sweet in the first instance, and have a trial run, to make sure that the rules are understood. Don't let an infringement occur without stopping the game and explaining, or everyone else will take it up too.

Equipment

Most of the equipment needed for these games is readily available; some games needing special gear have the details of how to make the necessary items beneath the game explanation.

Other equipment can easily be made:

<u>Soft balls</u>: some games call for a quantity of these. They are simple to make with a) cut-up stockings, b) cut-up sponge/foam chips, c) lightly-scrunched newspaper sheets. Pack in stocking-pieces, overwrapped two or three times to prevent leakage, then sew shut. Asking Mums for their old stockings or tights (washed!) will generally get you a good supply. Foam can be picked up from a number of sources. (I get my annual supply by going out into the street with a couple of bags after the Marathon's been run!).

The balls shouldn't be too tightly packed: a small handful of stocking-pieces, a larger handful of foam, or three single newspaper sheets, lightly scrunched, will make balls of adequate size and softness. The stocking and foam balls, apart from being washable, even bounce - though not necessarily in a straight line! These are much kinder on windows, lights, and heads than tennis balls.

<u>'Bashers'</u>: rolled-up newspapers, taped closed, make good 'bashers', and are fairly harmless when used by kids, although overdoing it should be discouraged. If only a few sheets of paper are used for each 'basher', they will be light enough to avoid serious injury!

<u>Blindfolds</u>: old material (sheets etc.) cut into foot-square pieces, over-wrapped to make them about three inches wide, and sewn shut, with a short length of elastic to go around the back of the head.

<u>Relay races</u>: we use batons which must be handed from one player to the next, to prevent false starts. These can be anything, even a bit of string!

THE GAMES

AIR MAIL **Compass/24 hour clock** **TR R T**

Each team has in front of it a heap of cards, with compass directions or degrees on each. Members of each team have a consecutive number. Establish North (point to a part of the hall and call that 'North'). All Number Ones take a card to the direction stated on it, relative to 'North'. Number Ones tag Number Twos, who do the same, and so on until all the cards are out.

If you colour-code or mark each set, it will a) make it easier to resort afterwards, and b) let you know which team is having particular trouble with its directions.

Variation: 24-hour clock - point out '12' and have cards in 24-hour time.

Equipment: set of cards per team, at least two per member.

BALLISTAE — Knots/lashings/thinking — T TR

Each team is given: several gardening canes of various lengths, none longer than three/four feet and some string. They have to build a catapult capable of throwing a soft ball to the end of the hall. There are many different types, depending upon age and ability. They might need a few hints - after they've tried by themselves!

While they're doing that, leaders build each team a pyramid of ten plastic beakers at the end of the hall. When the ballistae are complete, each team has several soft balls with which to try to knock down their pyramid.

Equipment: garden canes of various lengths, string, soft balls, plastic beakers

BALL SNATCH — T R XX

Divide the players into teams, and number. Each team is given a corner of the hall, or a section of wall for its base, and sits there. In the centre of the hall is a pile of small balls, sponges, etc. When a player's number is called, he has one minute to collect as many balls as he can, one at a time, from the centre stack and, when that is gone, from any other team's stack. Players taking from another team's stack must not be obstructed by that team. At the end of a minute, count up how many each team have, and put them all back into the centre and go again.

Equipment: small balls

BAT RACE **Hallowe'en** **R T**

Each player has a cut-out paper bat (perhaps made during a previous hand-craft session) and each team has a 'flapper' made from a piece of stiff card. Number Ones have to fan their bats, without touching them, down the hall. Then run back to hand the flapper to Number Two, etc., until all players' bats are over the finish line. First team home wins.

Equipment: 1 paper bat per boy; 1 'flapper' per team

BINBALL **R T XX**

Each team has a bowl/bin in front of it, with a chalked line some feet away (distance depending upon ability). Each player has a soft ball, and has to throw it so that it goes (and stays!) in the bin, on the relay system.

Equipment: 1 bowl/bin per team: 1 soft ball per player

BLANK YARN **Fun** **S Q**

Prepare a short story, leaving blanks instead of key words. Give players a card each, on which is written a word. Read the story - when you come to a blank, point to one of the players to read out his word. The results can be quite amusing. The same story and key-words can be used again, by varying the order in which players are picked out.

Example

One day, four children decided to go for a walk in the countryside. They met at [local spot] and waited at the bus stop. A -- came along, and they got on it and gave the conductor -- for their fares. When they reached the countryside, they got off and started walking through the fields. "A" saw a -- in a tree; they tried to feed it with a --, but it flew away.

They went on, closing all gates behind them, of course, and came to a stream. It had -- swimming in it, and they decided to stop and have their lunch. "A" had -- sandwiches, "B" had --, "C" had --, and "D" had --. Then they all had a drink of -- and went on, making sure that they hadn't left any litter behind them. "C" saw a herd of -- in a field, and they stopped to stroke them. After a while, they saw a farmer, who had a -- on a lead. The farmer gave them directions for reaching the main road, and they thanked him and walked on. It began to rain, so they put on their --, which they'd brought just in case. A -- came along, so they got on it and went home.

<u>Key-words</u> (Make them as unlikely as possible, or a fluke might happen and the word fit that particular gap in the story).

Policeman	Jumbo jet	Elephant
Welly boot	Brick	Polo Mint
Mars Bar	Bicycle Wheel	
Schoolteacher	Traffic Warden	
Polar Bear	Vicar	
Screwdriver		

Personalise with names and places known to the children. Make sure that you have enough words and blanks for everybody to have a go.

BLINDFOLD BOXING **Q S/T XX**

Sit the players in a large circle. Two are blindfolded and each is given a 'basher'. The object is to find, and hit, the other player without being hit oneself.

This can be played either as a solo or team game, with points awarded accordingly. As with all blindfold games, silence should be encouraged from the other players. This game does lead to some thrilling near misses which the spectators thoroughly enjoy.

Equipment: 2 blindfolds, 2 'bashers'

BUZZ **Teamwork** **T XX**

Two teams. Using a soft ball or beanbag, Team A has to get Team B out by hitting them below the knee. The players cannot move whilst in possession of the ball, but must pass it. The throwing side must learn not to keep chasing after the ball - and not to throw it just to their friends!

If numbers don't permit two teams, have a) members v leaders (either way) or b) one leader. As each player is 'out', he joins the leader's side, so that members are still in the game after they're 'dead'.

Equipment: soft ball

CAT AND MOUSE — L S X

Players form lines, fingertip-apart from the players on either side and from those in front and behind. Two players are left over: one is the Cat, the other the Mouse. The players put up their arms to form lines, and the Cat chases the Mouse without breaking the lines. Every now and then the leader calls 'Change' and the players swing through 90° and form lines going in the other direction.

Change the Cat and Mouse every now and then, to give them all a go.

CATERPILLAR RACE — Teamwork — T XX

Teams in line astern at one end of the hall. In front of them is a 'shark-infested' river which they must cross without touching the floor. Each team has a number of chairs, one less than the number of people in the team. The players get on to the chairs, and the last chair is passed to the front: they all move up one, and the empty chair is again passed to the front, until all the players and their chairs are over the finish line.

The biggest players should be first and last, since they'll have to pass the chairs: make sure that they don't space them too far for the smaller members to reach. Also make sure that the chairs are robust enough to stand the treatment they're likely to get!

You might rule that any player who touches the floor loses his team either a life or one of their chairs.

Equipment: Chairs, one less per team than members.

CENTIPEDE RACE | Teamwork | T XX

Each team takes a corner of the hall, and is supplied with bits of rope, one less than there are team-members. Number Ones run round the hall and back to their corners, where they join on with Number Twos and go round three-legged. Then the Number Threesjoin on, and so on until the whole team is tied together and has got round.

They should learn a bit about co-operation before they're finished! How about leaders doing it first, to show how 'easy' it really is? (Secret: if all the even numbers start on their right foot, and all the odd numbers start on their left, there should be no problem. See if they can work it out before you tell them!).

Equipment: short pieces of rope

CHAIN RACE | Knots | TR T R

Each team needs several lengths of rope, length depending upon the length of your meeting place. One piece per team is attached at one end of the hall, and the players relay, attaaching their rope until the team's rope extends the length of the hall and is attached to a chair or something similar.

The first team to complete their chain with correctly made knots wins. The knots can be specified for each player, or they can be general tying two ropes together knots.

Equipment: 1 rope per player

CHAIR FOOTBALL (i) **Handicapped** **T XX**

Split the players into two teams and tell them to take a chair, and to sit anywhere in the defined playing area. When they've done that, tell them that they're handicapped, confined to those chairs, and they're going to play football. Set up a couple of chairs each end for goals: teams must pass the ball down to score. They may use hands and feet, but mustn't rise from their chairs.

They'll probably not have much success at first, because they're sitting all over the place. After a while, let them relocate, and play on.

It wouldn't hurt to remind them that, at the end of the game, they at least can walk away!

Equipment: 1 chair per person, 1 large ball

CLEAR THE DECK **S X**

All the players walk round the hall. On the signal, they must all get off the floor. The last player gets a point; least points wins.

Equipment: none

CLIMBING MOUNT SNOWDON — R T XX

Teams in line astern at one end of the hall. The other end is the top of Mount Snowdon, and they have to climb up to it. Each team has a rope long enough to reach the length of the playing area, and Number One ropes up (with the proper knot!) and 'climbs' the north face of the hall floor - perhaps over and around obstacles.

When he's at the 'top', the others follow, one at a time (a chance to get across the proper climbing procedure) and follow wherever the rope goes. 'Rock slides' of small balls can be added from time to time. Extra points for realism!

Equipment: 1 long rope per team

COMMANDO CRICKET — T XX

Two teams. It's normal cricket, except that a) the bowling is continuous, whether the batsman's there or not, b) only the bowler can get the batsman out, c) the batsmen run to the side and back, not the front.

As soon as the bowler gets the ball, he bowls, whether the batsman's there or not. As soon as Batsman One is out, Number Two must take over immediately, because the bowler won't wait. The batsman can't run unless he hits the ball: then he <u>must</u> run. Bowling is underarm.

A ball caught one-handed means that the whole team is out; caught two-handed, only the batsman is out. If played indoors, rebounds from the wall, even if one-handed, don't count.

Players fielding must learn not to all keep chasing the ball. Players waiting to bat must keep back from the 'wicket'.

Equipment: bat (rounders/cricket) ball (soft if indoors), wicket - bin, box

CONFUSION — T X

Players are put into three teams. Each team is given an instruction <u>which the other teams must not know</u>: each team only knows what <u>it</u> has to do.

Team 1	Sit in a line in the centre of the hall, on chairs, and link arms.
Team 2	Prevent anyone from sitting on chairs in the centre of the hall.
Team 3	Remove all unoccupied chairs to the side of the hall. Prevent anyone taking them.

Stand well back before you give the signal to start! Let it go on for as long as you think fit. If all the teams are fairly evenly matched, nobody will win.

Variation: any set of mutually exclusive instructions, perhaps for more than 3 teams.

<u>Equipment</u>: chairs

<u>DARK DIALLING</u> **<u>Emergency procedure</u>** **<u>S TR</u>**

The players sit in a circle. In the middle is either a telephone, or a model dial. Each player in turn is blindfolded and has to a) find the phone, and b) dial 999. It can be expanded, with a leader being the Operator, into full emergency procedure.

It might be better if you can get hold of both the circular and push-button dials.

<u>Equipment</u>: telephone or model dial, blindfold

<u>DEFEND-YOUR-AREA</u> **<u>T XX</u>**

The hall is quartered, and the players divided into four teams, making sure if possible that sizes are evenly distributed. Each team takes a quarter of the hall: the object is to keep the ball out of one's own area, and to try to get it into somebody else's.

Every ten seconds a whistle is blown, and whoever's area the ball is in, or passing over, gets a point. Least points wins. Every few minutes, rotate the teams until they've all been in each quarter - this neutralises natural obstacles.

Anybody kicking the ball, or poaching another team's area, gets a penalty point. Depending upon the height of your ceiling, and the amount of protection on your lights, you might have to introduce a height limit for the ball.

The players must learn to spread out and cover the whole of their area, not all bunch at the front. It is possible, if a player's timing is right, for him to hold on to the ball, and drop it in another team's area just before the whistle blows, so that the other team don't have a chance to clear it, but good timing is essential!

<u>Equipment</u>: large ball

<u>DOMINOES</u> **<u>TR S/T</u>**

Prepare a set of dominoes on card, dealing with any subject you want to get over; the members take them, and play, as usual. First team out wins. If all the dominoes are correctly placed, you should end up with a complete, closed circle. It might help players to have a list to refer to in the beginning, but once they're a little better, they have to rely on memory.

Variations: morse, semaphore, mapping signs, compass (points and degrees), etc.

<u>Equipment</u>: dominoes

DUSTBINS R T

In front of each team, at the other end of the hall, is a pile of 'litter' - boxes, bits of paper, etc. Each player in turn goes and fetches a piece, and takes it to a chair behind the team (the 'dustbin') before tagging the next team member. The first team to have cleared all their litter wins.

Variation: have all the 'litter' in one big heap, and the team which picks up the most wins.

Equipment: 'litter', at least 2 pieces per member.

FIRST AID RACE — First Aid — T R TR

Each team is lined at one end of the hall. At the other end is a leader per team, and a stack of bandages. Number Ones come up and are told that 'their' leader has a cut finger, a sprained ankle etc. They have to treat the 'injury' with the gear available.

Variation: prepare a set of cards per team detailing injuries, up to the first aid level that players of that age should know. They take one each, and treat their leader accordingly.

Equipment: bandages of various types, set of cards per team

FRENCH LABELS **International** **T Q**

Prepare outline figures of a person, with various parts labelled - hand, eye, foot, etc. Each team is given one, and a list of corresponding French words; they must match the word to the feature. Compare afterwards.

Variation: any language - or rhyming slang!

Equipment: 1 chart and 1 list per team, pencils.

GRAB-BALL **T XX**

Chalk circles on the floor as in the sketch below. The second set should be about 1/3 of the way down the hall. The first set are the bases, and the second set, the targets. One player from each team acts as 'Runner', and operates between the two lines, while the rest of the team is in the greater part of the hall.

Soft balls are scattered about the hall. Players pick up the balls and put them in their team's target circle - all the players go together, but each may carry only one ball at a time. The Runner takes one ball at a time from the target and puts it in the base circle. He may only take balls from the target; if one rolls outside the circle, it's 'dead' until replaced inside the circle. Runners may raid each other's targets, one ball at a time, but not the bases. The team who collects the most balls within the time wins.

Equipment: soft balls

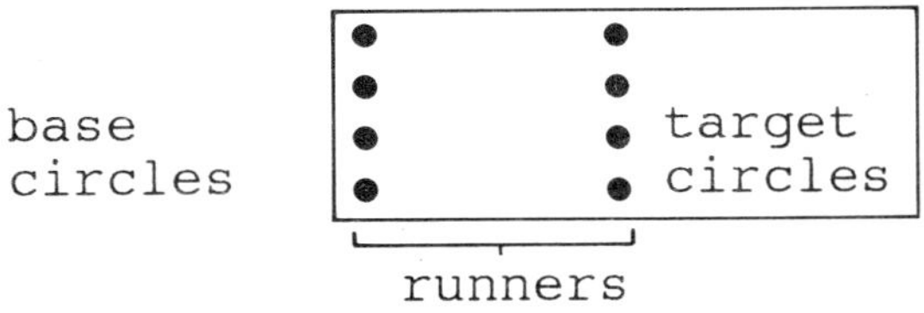

GUIDED TOUR (i) Local Knowledge TR S X

The players sit in a circle. The leader asks each one in turn for directions to a local street, or shop, or whatever. Can they give correct and precise directions?

Equipment: none

GUNGA-DIN T R XX

Set up a row of obstacles per team down the hall - tables and chairs. The teams are at one end of the hall. At the far end there should be a small bowl or jug; at the near end, a container of water. Each team is given one plastic beaker. Each player in turn has to fill the beaker and take it over the tables and under the chairs until he can empty it into the bowl - then straight back and hand it to the next player. The team to collect most water wins.

This is best not played in uniform or best clothes!

Equipment: tables, chairs, 1 plastic beaker per team, bowls, water containers.

HOPPIT S/T X

Two teams are numbered from alternate ends, and sit facing each other, about ten feet apart. When their number is called, each player folds his arms and hops out to the centre: the idea is to make the other player put both feet on the floor at once. Hoppers can change feet, as long as both aren't down together.

For the solo game, sit them in a circle and play the same way. Each team's victories are totalled at the end.

Equipment: none

INCIDENTS **TR T**

Each team is given a card detailing an incident: sprained ankle, finding a household fire, seeing someone shoplift, finding money in the street.

After a few moments to think about it, they act out the situation, and their response. This could be followed by general discussion: was it the right action? What do the others think could have been done?

Equipment: incident cards

JETLAG **S X**

The players stand in a circle with a leader, and hold hands. The leader squeezes the hand of the boy beside her; as soon as he feels the pressure, he sends it on until it gets back to the leader's other hand. Time how long it takes; this is a pretty good demonstration of reaction speed!

Equipment: none

KEEP AWAY **Teamwork** **L S XX**

All on to one. The Defender has a bat/tin plate etc. A soft ball is thrown from player to player until the Defender can be hit below the waist. The player who hit him then takes over.

Attacking can be done in one of two ways: passing the ball until it gets close enough; or a fielder can shout 'Freeze!' and everybody keeps still while he throws. If a fielder happens to be in his way, that's his hard luck.

Variation: when the players improve, start using two balls, from either side of the Defender.

Equipment: bat, soft ball

KILLING THE DRAGON — T X

Three players form the dragon: each holds on to the waist of the one in front, and the last player has a scarf tucked into the back of his belt for a 'tail'. The other players pair up. They piggyback to make St. George and his horse, and must try to kill the dragon by cutting off his tail. Make sure the 'horse' isn't bigger than 'St. George', or, when they swop, he won't be able to lift him!

Equipment: none

KIT RELAY — First Aid — T R TR

Prepare a set of cards per team, listing items to be found in a first aid kit. Put in several 'decoy' cards of items which don't belong.

Number Ones take a card, and place it in a 'Yes' or 'No' pile. When the whole team have had a go, they can compare their choices - you can then talk about what things they've put in or left out, asking them to justify their choices.

Equipment: set of cards per team

KNOT RACE **Knots** **TR R T XX**

The players form up into teams. Number Ones go to join the leader and are given a knot to tie, specified by type - i.e., a knot to join two pieces of rope, a knot to tie a sling, etc. The players must tie the correct knot for that purpose. When they've done it, they tag Number Two, and so on.

Equipment: short lengths of rope

LADDERS **T X**

Two teams, sized according to running ability. They face each other, then sit, their legs out and feet touching those of the opposing player. Number the pairs going away from the leader. When a number is called, the players run over the legs away from the leader, round two chairs at the end (this prevents them from swinging round the last pair), down the outside, round two more chairs, and back over the legs to their place. The first to be sitting properly wins the point.

The pairs should be spaced a couple of feet apart - enough to accommodate players of differing strides without them treading on anyone. For safety's sake, players MUST keep their legs together and down while others are running.

After running through once, you might have to swop players to match up those of differing abilities, so that they're more evenly paired.

Equipment: none

LETTER HUNT   Observation   S XX TR

Give each player or team a pencil and paper. Tell them to go round the meeting place, listing every item they can find beginning with a certain letter, which you tell them. See who can get the longest list.

Equipment: pencils/paper

THE LOOKING-OVER   Jungle Book   O S XX

Explain the Jungle Book story, 'the looking-over'. Then blindfold one player: the others spread out, and he has to catch one. The caught player then growls, and the blindfolded one has to say who it is. If he's right, the caught player takes over.

Equipment: blindfold

MAP SNAP   Local Knowledge/maps   TR S

Prepare two sets of cards, one with a portion of a local map showing a local building (or O.S. map symbol) and the other set with the name of the building (or symbol). Shuffle and deal them out to the players, who sit in a circle and play Snap, trying to match the building's site and its name, or the map symbol and its name.

Equipment: set of snap cards

MEMORY CHASE | **Memory** | **TR T R XX**

Teams at one end of the hall, each with tables and chairs in front of it. Number One goes over the obstacles, and is given one word of a message. He goes back over the course and whispers it to Number Two ONLY; Number Two then runs the course and is given a second word, which he passes with the first word on to Number Three, and so on. At the end, see what the message emerges as!

Equipment: tables/chairs

MIMES | **Help other people** | **L O S**

Prepare a set of cards detailing ways in which the players can help other people. The first player takes a card and mimes it; the one who guesses the activity takes the next, and so on.

Suggestions: gardening, shopping, brushing the dog, baby-sitting, giving up a seat on a bus, holding a door open, washing-up, etc.

Equipment: mime cards

NETS — T X

Two players link wrists to make a Net. The others are the Fish. They are caught by the Net dropping over their heads, and they then join the Net. When a fourth player is caught, they split to become two Nets, and so on until only one Fish is left.

Equipment: none

NUMBER BALL (i) — XX

The players stand in a large circle. In the middle is a leader with a large ball. She throws it to each player in turn, counting the catch and return as 'one', 'two' etc. The idea is to see how high a score the players can reach without the ball being dropped; then the count starts again from 'one'. Nobody wins or loses: each player is trying his hardest for the whole team.

Equipment: large ball

NUMBERS (i) — S X

The players walk round the hall. Every now and then, the leader calls a number, and the players have to get into groups of that number: any groups over or under are out, as are any left-over players.

It takes quite a bit of juggling to ensure that only one or two people are out each time! Try calling out 'one' now and then and watch what they do!

Equipment: none

ODD-BALL Throwing/catching S XX

The players may either form a circle or a line. The leader throws a large ball to each. If it's caught, and returned, the player takes a step back. If it's dropped, or thrown in such a way that the leader can't catch it, he takes a step forward. The player furthest away at the end of time wins.

Equipment: large ball

OVER AND UNDER (i) R T XX

The teams form up line astern. Each has a large ball. Number Ones pass it over their heads to Number Twos, who pass it between their legs to Number Three, and so on, over and under to the last player, who runs to the front, and passes it over to Number One, etc.

The first team to be formed up as they were at the beginning wins. The teams will tend to 'scrunch up' as the game goes on, so move them out a bit.

Equipment: 1 large ball per team

ONE HAND TWO HANDS S XX

The players stand in a large circle, a leader in the centre with a ball. She throws it to them in turn. On their first drop, they go to one knee, on their second, both knees, on their third, one hand behind their backs, and fourth drop is out.

If a player catches the ball after having previously dropped it, he goes back to his previous position; if he was on both knees, he goes on to one.

<u>Equipment</u>: large ball

<u>PAPER ROUND</u> <u>Local Knowledge</u> <u>TR S</u>

This will need advance preparation. Prepare a st of cards, each in two parts; the first giving a local point (fire station, baker's shop) and the second telling them to go to another location. Each card is stuck on the wall in the direction that the shop is (if the fire station is north of the hall, it goes on the north wal). From there they are sent to another location, and so on round.

Each card carries a letter, and if all cards are visited in the correct order, a word is spelled out. So the boys have to know where each named place is located to be able to go round in the correct order.

<u>Equipment</u>: prepared cards

<u>PIT STOP</u> <u>T X</u>

Like 'Zoos' (cf) but with racing-car theme. The teams all have racing-car names: Lotus, Ferrari, ~~etc~~. McLaren

'On the grid' - into line astern sitting.
'Chequered flag' - all the team runs.
'Pit stop' - all the team on their backs, hands and feet in the air to get their tyres changed. 'On the grid' gets them back into line.
Get Set - Jogg on spot

<u>Equipment</u>: none
Race - run about

PUPPETS T R

Each team will need a pair of 'stilts' (tin cans or blocks with a length of string attached to both sides of each, long enough so that, when the player stands on the tins, he has to hold his hands above his head, hence the title).

A stack of soft balls is put at the other end of the hall per team. Number Ones stand on the cans, hold the 'reins', and walk themselves down the hall, pick up a ball, and return with it. Then Number Twos, and so on. The first team to pick up their stack wins.

Variation: real stilts! Just going to the end of the hall and back will be quite enough.

Equipment: two tins/blocks per team, 'reins', soft balls

"QUIET" GAME T X

It isn't! Two teams, one of which is halved and placed at either end of the hall. The other team is between the split team. Team A have to pass a message verbally to the other half of their team; Team B have to prevent them simply by making as much noise as they can. When Team A think they've got the message, they put their hands up.

This is best not played for too long, to save people's hearing!

Equipment: none

RELAY CHUCK — Catching/throwing — T XX TR

Each team is spread out along the length of the hall, and a stack of soft balls put down by each Number One. They have to throw the balls to each other, down the line. The first team to get all their balls to the the other end of the hall wins. Dropped balls go back to Number One.

Equipment: soft balls

ROLLABALL — L S XX

The players form a large circle, with one in the centre. The object is to pass the ball from one side of the circle to the other without the centre player getting it. If he does, the one who last rolled it goes into the centre.

Equipment: large ball

ROUNDUP — T

Teams of Cowboys have to round-up their herds of cattle (cards marked with various 'brands', which have been hidden around the area). Each team must leave one player on guard at their base to protect the cattle they've already collected, otherwise the Rustlers (leaders) will make off with the herd. Each player may only bring back one card at a time, and only their own brand (unofficial Rustlers will be hung!).

The team with the largest herd of unrustled cattle wins.

The guard should change every now and then, to give all the players a chance to go out.

Equipment: 'brand' cards, at least 3 per player, 1 set per team

SCRAMBLE S X

Stand the players in a fairly small circle, so that they're within reach of each other. Each has to hold the wrist or ankle of the boy beside him, while trying to prevent his own wrist or ankle from being held.

To begin with, it's easier if they go for the left wrist/ankle of the player on their right, and the right wrist/ankle of the player on their left. Once they've got that, you could make it the right limb of the person on their right, or the next but one player.

Shoes should be removed before playing, for safety.

Equipment: none

SHIP ON THE ROCKS   S X

One end of the hall is Port, the other Starboard. The players have to do the appropriate action when the key-word is called. Calling 'Port' when they're already at Port can be amusing!

Captain's coming aboard	-	alert and salute
Climb the rigging	-	mime climbing
Boom's coming over	-	flat on floor, hands on head
Ship's sinking	-	on their backs, feet in the air
Submarine	-	on their backs, arm up for periscope
Scrub the decks	-	on BOTH knees, scrubbing
Freeze	-	stand perfectly still
Look-out	-	standing, miming look-out

And any others you might think of!

Equipment: none

SLEIGH RIDE (i)   Knots   R T XX

Each team has a small table or chair upturned at the other end of the hall. Number Ones come out and are told to tie a specified knot around one of the legs. When it's done correctly he tags Number Two, until there are as many ropes on the table/chair as there are players in the team.

When that's done, the sleigh is hitched up, and the players run out and tow it home by the ropes. It's best to have one leader per team, to check on the accuracy of the knotting.

Equipment: lengths of string or rope, 1 table/chair per team

SNATCH THE HAT (i) T XX

Two teams sit on opposite sides of the hall. Size and number them from alternate ends. In the centre is a hat/small ball. When a number is called, the players have to come out, get the hat, and get back to their own line without being tagged. They can't be tagged until they've picked up the ball.

Equipment: hat/small ball

SNOWBALL FIGHT T

Each team has an equal number of Snowballs (scrunched-up paper sheets) and an equal area of hall. The idea is to get rid of one's own snowballs, and to keep other teams out of your area. Stop every now and then to count up and redistribute. This can be played by any number of teams at once.

Equipment: 'Snowballs'

SPACE-SHIP-ON-THE-ROCKS — S X

As 'Ship-on-the-rocks' (cf), but with different key-words:

Asteroids	look-out
Meteors	flat on the floor, hands on head
Space-suits on	mime climbing into space-suits
Captain's coming	alert and salute
EVA	Space-walk (slow-motion!)
Accelerate	on back on floor, still
Blast-off	on back on floor, knees raised.

Equipment: none

SPOT THE CHANGE — Observation — S X TR

Start the meeting off as usual. While everybody is busy with another activity, make some slight alteration to your uniform. Don't tell the players. At the end, ask if anyone's noticed what's different - once they know that they were supposed to see something, they'll probably spot it! Then point out that you were like that for the whole meeting, and only (name the players who <u>did</u> spot it - if any did) saw it - and their eyes are just the same as everyone else's!

Equipment: none

STAMP COLLECTING **Observation** **S XX**

Take a postage stamp, and attach it to your person. Then go on with whatever activity is scheduled. See how long it takes for anyone to notice! Or tell them that a stamp has been put somewhere, in plain sight (if they look in the right direction). As boys see it, they sit down withot telling anyone else where it is!

Equipment: postage stamp or small sticker

SQUASH FOOTBALL **S XX**

Suitable for a small number of players. One-touch football against a wall; each player kicks it, and the next one must also kick it before it hits the opposite wall. If he fails, then he gets a point. Least points wins. If a player kicks it, but it doesn't reach the target wall, then he also gets a point. The ball may be kicked anywhere along the target wall to make the next person run for it.

Equipment: large ball

STAFF SWOP — S XX

Each player has a staff, about chin-height. They stand in a fairly small circle, and stand the staff in front of them, holding it with their open palm on top of it. When the leader says "left" or "right", they let go of their staff and move in the indicated direction, catching hold of the staff next to them on their left or right before it hits the ground.

As they get better, you can move the circle out a bit. If the leader says "left-left" or "right-right", they have to go to the next-but-one staff.

It's best if they hold the staves in the way I've described: if they hold it in their fist, they tend to 'throw' it away from them as they move round. With their hand flat on top, they only have to lift it.

Equipment: 1 staff per boy

SWING BRIDGE — S X

Chalk a number of circles (about 2'diameter) on the floor. They're the swing bridges. The players walk around, and every now and then the leader blows a whistle. That's the signal that the swing bridges are opening, and any player inside one of the circles is drowned!

Equipment: none

SNATCH THE BOTTLE T XX

Divide the players into two teams, and sit them facing the other with a wide space between. Number from alternate ends. In the gap between the teams, place five washing-up liquid bottles. When a number is called, the players have to fetch one bottle at a time back to their line - they must not throw them down. The one to get the fifth bottle gets the point.

Equipment: 5 plastic bottles

TIGHTROPE T XX

Upend two tables, about ten feet apart. You'll need a length of rope, eyed at both ends, or knotted into loops. The tables should be spread far enough apart that if the loop at one end is put over one table-leg, the other loop won't reach the second table. It helps to have a couple of leaders standing on the tables to keep them still.

Put the players into two teams against either side, and number them. When a number is called, the player with that number has to get the loop over his team's table-leg. As the rope isn't long enough for both, this can result in quite a tug-of-war. The player who gets his loop over wins the point.

Equipment: 2 tables, 1 rope, looped/eyed at each end.

TOWERS **Manual Dexterity** **S XX**

Put a stack of plastic beakers in the centre of the hall. Each player has to build a tower, as high as he can, taking one beaker at a time from the central stack. The highest tower at the end of time wins - not the tower that would have been the highest if it hadn't just collapsed!

Equipment: plastic beakers

TRAY FOOTBALL **T R**

For this game you will need metal trays (serving trays, oven trays, etc), one per team, or one per player if you can get enough, and have few enough players.

If you have only a few trays, play the relay version. Number the teams and put them to each side of the hall, goals at each end. When a player's number is called, he sits on the tray, skates out, and tries to score.

If you have enough trays, you could play it as a full team game.

Equipment: 1 metal tray per team, football

TREASURE CHEST   T R

For this you need old padlocks, with keys, and some old keys. Give each team a handful of keys, and put a closed padlock at the other end of the hall. Each player selects a key and tries to open the padlock. First team to succeed wins.

Equipment: padlock per team, variety of keys

(NB Make sure you can find the right keys afterwards)

TUNNEL BALL   R T XX

The players form up in teams, line astern, spread out a bit. Their feet should be widely spread. Number Ones have a large ball,l which they roll down the line. Last players pick it up, run to the front, and repeat until the Number Ones are again at the front.

The teams tend to bunch up, so spread them out again - perhaps making two marks, one for the first player to stand on, and one for the player at the back.

Equipment: large ball per team

WELLY SCRAMBLE **T**

Divide the players into two teams, matching sizes and strengths. Sit them facing about ten/twelve feet apart, and number from alternate ends. Mark off the playing area between them with chalk, an old blanket, etc (we use a couple of judo mats, side by side).

In the centre of the playing area, place three large (adult) wellies. When a number is called, the players with that number each put on one welly, step completely out of the playing area, then go back for the third welly. Whoever manages to get both wellies on and out of the playing area at any point wins.

Strategy is useful - if a player is clutching one welly tightly to his chest, his opponent can go for the welly he's wearing, etc.

These rules MUST be obeyed: NO handing round necks, kicking, or punching; 'Stop' means INSTANTLY. If the game's gone on for a while, call it a draw and let another pair have a go.

THIS IS NOT A GAME FOR PLAYERS WHO HAVE TO 'WIN AT ALL COSTS'!

Equipment: 3 adult wellies, blanket or similar

WHAT'S THE TIME, MR. WOLF? **S X**

A traditional game. All the players are at one of the hall, except for one in the centre - he's the wolf. The players say 'What's the time, Mr. Wolf?' and he says various times. When he says 'Dinner time!' they have to run to the other end of the hall without being tagged.

You can play either that the first player who's tagged becomes the new wolf, or that every player tagged joins the wolf, and the last player caught becomes the wolf in the next game.

N.B. A touch is all that's needed!

Equipment: none

WITCH HUNT **S L Q XX**

One player is blindfolded, and must catch the others, who are only allowed to take three steps per game. Once they've taken them, they may duck and dodge, but must keep their feet still. Anyone caught becomes the new witch-finder.

Equipment: blindfold

ZOOM **T X**

Four teams, one in each corner of the hall. If the leader calls "One", they move to the next corner clockwise. If the leader calls "Two", they move to the next corner anti-clockwise. And if "Three" is called, they move to the diagonally opposite corner.

Once they've got the hang of it, call out sequences of numbers: ie, "2 3 1 2". The players do not do each action in turn - instead, they have to work out where they would end up, and go straight there.

Equipment: none

INDEX

S — Solo games - each boy against all the others

T — Team games

R — Relay games

L — Loop games - no winners, no losers, the game just goes on

Tr — Training games (training in its wider sense of learning skills)

Q — Quiet games

XX — Games for which no special equipment is needed. (If the place that you meet in is anything like mine, then such gear as these games require will be readily available - tables, chairs, ball etc.)

X — Games for which no equipment at all is needed

PAGE	GAME	CODE							
		S	T	R	L	Tr	Q	X	XX
14	CHAIN RACE		x	x		x			
15	CHAIR FOOTBALL		x						x
15	CLEAR THE DECK	x						x	
16	CLIMBING MOUNT SNOWDON		x	x					x
16	COMMANDO CRICKET		x						x
17	CONFUSION		x						x
18	DARK DIALLING	x				x			
18	DEFEND-YOUR-AREA		x						x
19	DOMINOES	x	x			x			
20	DUSTBINS		x	x					
20	FIRST AID RACE		x	x		x			
21	FRENCH LABELS		x				x		
21	GRAB BALL		x						x
22	GUIDED TOUR	x				x		x	
22	GUNGA DIN					x			x
23	HOPPIT	x	x				x		
24	INCIDENTS		x			x			
24	JETLAG	x						x	
24	KEEP AWAY	x			x				x
25	KILLING THE DRAGON		x					x	
25	KIT RELAY		x	x		x			
26	KNOT RACE		x	x		x			x
26	LADDERS		x					x	
27	LETTER HUNT	x				x		x	
27	THE LOOKING-OVER	x					x		x
27	MAP SNAP	x	x						
28	MEMORY CHASE		x	x		x			x
28	MIMES	x			x		x		
29	NETS		x					x	
29	NUMBER BALL (i)								x
29	NUMBERS (i)	x						x	
30	ODD-BALL	x							x
30	OVER AND UNDER (i)		x	x					x
30	ONE HAND TWO HANDS	x							x
31	PAPER ROUND	x				x			

PAGE	GAME	CODE							
		S	T	R	L	Tr	Q	X	XX
31	PIT STOP		x					x	
32	PUPPETS		x	x					
32	"QUIET" GAME		x					x	
33	RELAY CHUCK		x			x			x
33	ROLLABALL	x			x				x
33	ROUNDUP		x						
34	SCRAMBLE	x						x	
35	SHIP ON THE ROCKS	x						x	
35	SLEIGH RIDE (i)		x	x					x
36	SNATCH THE HAT (i)		x						x
36	SNOWBALL FIGHT		x						
37	SPACE-SHIP-ON-THE ROCKS	x						x	
37	SPOT THE CHANGE	x				x		x	
38	STAMP COLLECTING	x							x
38	SQUASH FOOTBALL	x							x
39	STAFF SWOP	x							x
39	SWING BRIDGE	x						x	
40	SNATCH THE BOTTLE		x						x
40	TIGHTROPE		x						x
41	TOWERS	x							x
41	TRAY FOOTBALL		x	x					
42	TREASURE CHEST		x	x					
42	TUNNEL BALL		x	x					x
43	WELLY SCRAMBLE		x						
43	WHAT'S THE TIME MR. WOLF?	x						x	
44	WITCH HUNT	x			x		x		x
44	ZOOM		x					x	